Summary

The Obama Administration released the President's FY2012 budget proposal on February 14, 2011. According to the Administration's estimates, the tax proposals in the budget would increase revenues $280 billion over the next 10 years. The Administration's estimates were made relative to a current policy budget baseline, which assumes certain polices that are scheduled to change in the future by law will not. In contrast, the Congressional Budget Office (CBO) and Joint Committee on Taxation (JCT) make their projections relative to a current law budget baseline, which assumes future policy changes will occur as prescribed by current laws. This difference in baselines may result in the Administration's estimates being different than future CBO and JCT estimates.

This report provides a broad overview of the provisions included in the President's budget request. The budget groups proposed tax provisions into several general categories. The Administration estimates the net budgetary impact of the proposals in each category as follows:

- Tax cuts for families and individuals would reduce revenues by $92.0 billion over 5 years and $253.6 billion over 10 years.

- Tax cuts for business would reduce revenues by $46.6 billion over 5 years and $116.4 billion over 10 years.

- Tax incentives to promote regional growth would reduce revenues by $4.7 billion over 5 years and $5.3 billion over 10 years.

- Extending certain expiring tax provisions through 2012 would reduce revenues by $21.7 billion over 5 years and 22.3 billion over 10 years.

- Reducing certain tax expenditures to pay for three years of AMT relief would increase revenues by $113.9 billion over 5 years and $321.3 billion over 10 years.

- Other revenue changes and provisions the proposal terms loophole closers would increase revenues by $166.2 billion over 5 years and $356.5 billion over 10 years.

Congress has begun its consideration of the President's budget. The House and Senate Budget Committees are responsible for formulating and reporting an annual budget resolution. The budget committees typically develop the budget resolution as they receive information and testimony from various sources, such as the Administration, CBO, and congressional committees with jurisdiction over spending and revenues. The timetable established in the Congressional Budget Act directs the Senate Budget Committee to report a budget resolution by April 1 and for the House and Senate to reach final agreement on a budget resolution by April 15.

I0447401

Contents

Tables

Contacts

Introduction

On February 14, 2011, the Administration released the President's FY2012 budget proposal.[1] This report provides a broad overview of the proposed tax provisions in the budget. Also provided are the Administration's 5- and 10-year revenue estimates for individual tax proposal line-items.[2]

Tax Cuts for Families and Individuals

The tax cuts for individuals and families that are proposed in the President's budget would expand and extend certain middle-income tax relief while allowing tax cuts for upper-income taxpayers to expire. Overall, the Administration estimates that the proposed tax cuts for families and individuals would reduce revenues by $92.0 billion over 5 years and $253.6 billion over 10 years.

Expand Earned Income Tax Credit

Beginning in 2013, the President's budget would make permanent the expansion in eligibility for the Earned Income Tax Credit (EITC) that was originally part of the American Recovery and Reinvestment Act of 2009 (ARRA; P.L. 111-5). For tax years 2009 and 2010, ARRA increased the maximum credit amount from $4,824 to $5,657 for working families with three or more children. This translated into an increase in the maximum credit rate for this group of families from 40% to 45%. The Tax Relief, Unemployment Insurance Reauthorization, and Job Creation Act of 2010 (P.L. 111-312) extended the ARRA modifications through 2012.[3]

Expand Child and Dependent Care Tax Credit

Taxpayers may currently claim a nonrefundable tax credit to partially offset child and dependent care expenses. The credit is equal to 35% of up to $3,000 of eligible expenses for one child or dependent, and up to $6,000 of eligible expenses for more than one child. The credit rate decreases by one percentage point for every $2,000 of adjusted gross income (AGI) over $15,000 until the percentage of expenses for which it may be claimed reaches 20% (at incomes above $43,000).

The President's budget proposes to increase the income level at which the credit rate begins to decrease from $15,000 to $75,000 beginning in 2012. Under the President's proposal the 35% credit rate would decrease by one percentage point for every $2,000 of AGI over $75,000 until the credit rate reached 20% (at incomes above $103,000).

---

[1] U.S. Office of Management and Budget, *Budget of the United States Government, Fiscal Year 2012*, at http://www.whitehouse.gov/omb/budget.

[2] The tax-related proposals discussed in this report are listed in Table S-2 of the FY2012 budget. Ibid., pp. 183-187, at http://www.whitehouse.gov/sites/default/files/omb/budget/fy2012/assets/tables.pdf

[3] For detailed information see CRS Report RS21352, *The Earned Income Tax Credit (EITC): Changes for 2011 and 2012*, by Christine Scott.

Automatic Enrollment In IRAs, Employer Enrollment Tax Credit, and Small Employer Plan Tax Credit

The President's budget proposes to require employers (except those with fewer than 10 employees and those in business for less than two years) who do not currently offer a retirement plan to offer automatic enrollment in an IRA to all employees beginning in 2013.[4] The employee automatic enrollment contribution would be 3% of employee compensation. The IRS has previously issued rulings that allow employers to automatically enroll employees in employee-sponsored retirement plans. Currently, employees must be notified of the enrollment in advance and permitted to leave the plan at their discretion.

The President's budget also proposes offering employers that participate in automatic enrollment a temporary business tax credit for two years equal to $25 per participating employee up to $250 per year.

The President's budget also proposes doubling a temporary business tax credit available to small employers (those with no more than 100 employees) who sponsor a qualified retirement plan or SIMPLE plan. Currently, small employers can claim a tax credit equal to 50% of the startup cost of sponsoring a plan. The maximum credit is $500 a year for three years. The President's proposal would increase the maximum credit from $500 to $1,000 per year for three years beginning in 2013.

Extend the American Opportunity Tax Credit

The President's budget proposes permanently extending the American Opportunity Tax Credit (AOTC)—a tax benefit for post secondary education—and indexing the eligible expense and income limits for inflation beginning in 2013.[5] The AOTC, which temporarily replaces the Hope credit, was first made available by ARRA for 2009 and 2010. It was extended through 2012 by the Tax Relief, Unemployment Insurance Reauthorization, and Job Creation Act of 2010 (P.L. 111-312). The AOTC allows taxpayers to claim a maximum $2,500 credit for tuition and related expenses (including books). Unlike the Hope credit, which is only available for the first two years of college, the AOTC is available for the first four years of college. In addition, 40% of the AOTC is refundable. The credit is gradually reduced for taxpayers with modified adjusted gross income between $80,000 and $90,000 (between $160,000 and $180,000 if married). Households with modified adjusted gross income above $90,000 ($180,000 if married) are ineligible for the credit.

Exclude Forgiven Student Loan Debt from Income

The President's budget proposes excluding from income certain student loan debt that is currently subject to income tax beginning in 2012. Currently, taxpayers who participate in one of two income-related repayment options offered by the Federal Family Loan and Federal Direct Loan

---

[4] For more information about automatic enrollment in 401(k) plans see, CRS Report RS21954, *Automatic Enrollment in 401(k) Plans*, by John J. Topoleski.

[5] For more information about the AOTC and other tax benefits for higher education, see CRS Report RL32554, *An Overview of Tax Benefits for Higher Education Expenses*, by Mark P. Keightley.

programs must pay tax on any loan amount that is forgiven at the end repayment period. Under the two options available, taxpayers make payments for either 25 years or 10 years (the shorter repayment period is for those working in a qualified public service position). Any loan balance remaining at the end of repayment period is forgiven, but considered taxable income. The President's proposal would apply to loan balances that remain at the end of the two income repayment related options.

Tax Capital Gains and Dividends of Certain Taxpayers at 20%

The President's budget proposes a 20% tax rate on capital gains and dividends for single taxpayers earning over $200,000 and for married taxpayers earning over $250,000.[6] Prior to 2003, capital gains were taxed at a rate of 20% or 10% depending on one's income. A maximum 18% rate was applied to gains realized on assets held over five years. In addition, dividends were taxed as ordinary income, and therefore subject to the marginal income tax schedule (maximum rate of 39.6%). In 2003, JGTRRA, initially lowered the rates of taxation on these forms of income to 15% or 10% (again, depending on one's income), and eventually lowered the 10% rate to 0% beginning in 2008. The Tax Increase Prevention and Reconciliation Act of 2005 (TIPRA; P.L. 109-222) extended these rate reductions through the end of 2010. The rates were extended again through 2012 by the Tax Relief, Unemployment Insurance Reauthorization, and Job Creation Act of 2010 (P.L. 111-312). The President's baseline assumes that the 15% and 0% rates will be permanently extended for middle-class taxpayers. The President's proposal would also repeal the maximum 18% rate on longer-held assets.

Tax Cuts for Businesses

The tax cuts for businesses that are proposed in the President's budget focus primarily on enhancing the research and experimentation tax credit and expanding the tax incentives for energy investment and manufacturing. Overall, the Administration estimates that the proposed tax incentives for businesses reduce revenues by $46.6 billion over 5 years and $116.4 billion over 10 years.

Eliminate Taxation of Capital Gains on Investments in Qualified Small Business Stock

Under Internal Revenue Code (IRC) Section 1202, non-corporate investors who acquire small business stock at first issue after September 27, 2010, and before January 1, 2012, and hold it for a minimum of five years, may exclude 100% of any gain they realize from the sale or exchange of the stock. The excluded gain for stock acquired during this period is not considered a preference item under the alternative minimum tax (AMT). For qualified stock acquired between February 18, 2009, and September 27, 2010, the exclusion drops to 75%; but the excluded gains are subject to the AMT. The exclusion reverts to its original level for stock acquired in 2012 and later: 50%. To qualify for the exclusion, the stock must be issued by a C corporation with gross

---

[6] For detailed information, see CRS Report R40411, *The Economic Effects of Capital Gains Taxation*, by Thomas L. Hungerford and CRS Report RL31597, *The Taxation of Dividend Income: An Overview and Economic Analysis of the Issues*, by Jane G. Gravelle.

assets of $50 million or less that is involved in a trade or business outside banking and finance, farming, food and lodging, oil and gas extraction, professional sports, the performing arts, business services (including accounting), health care, law, and architecture.

The President's budget proposes to permanently extend the 100% exclusion for gains on the sale of small business stock and to permanently eliminate the excluded gain as an AMT preference item, as of January 1, 2012. No other changes in the rules governing the use of the exclusion would be made, with one exception. Taxpayers claiming the exclusion would be required to submit additional information to the Internal Revenue Service (IRS) to ensure they are complying with those rules.

Enhance and Permanently Extend the Research and Experimentation Tax Credit

Under IRC Section 41, companies engaging in or financing qualified research may claim a nonrefundable credit. The credit has four components: (1) a regular credit equal to 20% of qualified research expenditures (QREs) above a base amount linked to a company's ratio of QREs to gross receipts in three of the years from 1984 to 1988, or to 3% of current-year QREs in the case of start-up companies; (2) an alternative simplified credit (ASC) equal to 14% of QREs that exceed 50% of a company's average annual QREs in the three previous tax years, and for companies with no QREs in any of those years, the credit is equal to 6% of current-year QREs; (3) a 20% credit for payments above a base amount to universities to conduct basic research; and (4) a flat 20% credit for payments to consortia engaged in energy research. In the case of the regular credit, the base amount cannot be less than 50% of current-year QREs. The research and experimentation credit, which has been extended 14 times, is due to expire on December 31, 2011. It has an incremental design for the purpose of giving companies an added incentive to undertake more QRE than they otherwise would.

The President's budget proposes to permanently extend the credit and increase the rate for the ASC from 14% to 17%, starting January 1, 2012. These changes may address what critics say are two critical problems with the regular credit: its lack of permanence and a weak incentive effect.[7]

Tax Credit for Investment in Advanced Energy Property

The advanced energy manufacturing tax credit (IRC § 48C) was established under ARRA to encourage investment in domestic clean-energy manufacturing. Under ARRA, $2.3 billion was allocated for tax credits, which were competitively awarded. Projects receiving an award could claim a 30% tax credit for qualified investments in advanced energy manufacturing. Projects were selected based on a broad range of criteria, including commercial viability, potential for domestic job creation, and potential for technological innovation. More than 500 applications, totaling $8 billion in tax credit requests, were received. Ultimately, 183 projects were selected to receive the $2.3 billion that was allocated for this project. The President's budget proposes authorizing an additional $5 billion for Section 48C tax credits.

---

[7] For more information, see CRS Report RL31181, *Research Tax Credit: Current Law, Legislation in the 112th Congress, and Policy Issues* , by Gary Guenther

Tax Credit for Energy Efficient Commercial Building Expenditures

Under current law, taxpayers are allowed a deduction for certain energy-efficiency improvements to commercial building property. A deduction of up to $1.80 per square foot is allowed for qualifying improvements to (1) the interior lighting system; (2) the heating, cooling, ventilation, and hot water system; and (3) the building envelope. A partial deduction is available for improvements made to a single system. The President's budget proposes to enhance the current tax incentives for commercial building energy efficiency by replacing the existing tax deduction with a tax credit. The tax credit would be available for property placed in service during calendar year 2012.

Incentives to Promote Regional Growth

The tax incentives to promote regional growth that are proposed in the President's budget would expand existing regional development programs. Overall, the Administration's proposals to promote regional growth would reduce revenues by $4.7 billion over 5 years and $5.3 billion over 10 years.

Extend and Modify the New Markets Tax Credit (NMTC)

The NMTC is intended to stimulate a greater flow of equity capital into low-income and economically distressed areas by giving investors a tax incentive to invest in community development entities (CDEs). These entities, in turn, are required to invest at least 85% of their tax-preferred capital in projects intended to promote the development of qualified low-income communities. CDEs are certified by a branch of the Treasury Department (the Community Development Financial Institutions Fund or CDFI), and they compete for the right to receive tax-preferred investments.

The NMTC is a nonrefundable tax credit equal to 39% of qualified equity investments (QEIs) in corporations or partnerships that qualify as CDEs. A QEI is an acquisition of stock (in the case of a corporation) or a capital interest (in the case of a partnership) in a CDE that is held for seven years. There is a limit on the share of the credit that a taxpayer can take in each year of that period: 5% of the amount invested in the CDE in the year the investment is made and the following two years, and 6% in each of the next four years, which sum to 39% after seven years. There is also an annual limit on the total amount of tax-preferred investment eligible for the credit. Through the end of 2010, the CDFI has authorized $31 billion in tax-preferred financing; another $5 billion is available for 2011. The NMTC can be used to offset tax liability under the regular income tax but not under the alternative minimum tax (AMT). It is due to expire on December 31, 2011.[8]

The President's budget proposes to extend the NMTC for one year (through the end of 2012) with another allocation of $5 billion. In addition, the proposal would allow any credit taken for QEIs made in 2011 and 2012 to offset AMT liability. These changes would become effective on the date of enactment.

---

[8] For more information about the NMTC program, see CRS Report RL34402, *New Markets Tax Credit: An Introduction*, by Donald J. Marples.

Reform and Expand the Build America Bonds

The President's budget proposal would make the Build America Bonds (BAB) program permanent and lower the credit rate to 28% from the previous 35% rate.[9] The FY2012 budget proposal would also relax the requirement that direct payment BABs (where the issuer receives the tax credit, not the investor) be used only for capital projects. The authority to issue BABs had expired December 31, 2010. Before expiration, $181.2 billion of BABs were issued or roughly one-fifth of total issuance.[10]

Reform and Expand the Low-Income Housing Tax Credit Program

The President's budget proposes amending the rent restriction requirements of the low-income housing tax credit (LIHTC) program. Currently, to qualify for the LIHTC program a property owner must choose between one of two rent restriction requirements: (1) at least 20% of the units must be rent restricted and occupied by tenants with income at or below 50% of area median income (AMI); or at least 40% of the units must be rent restricted and occupied by tenants with incomes at or below 60% of AMI.[11]

The President's budget proposes adding a third choice, which would require that at least 40% of LIHTC units be occupied by tenants with incomes that *average* no more than 60% of AMI. The pool of tenants used to compute this average could not include any tenant with an income over 80% of AMI. In addition, for purposes of computing the average, any tenant whose income is less than 20% of AMI would be treated as if their income were 20% of AMI.

Also included in the President's budget is a proposal to provide a 30% increase in the basis of LIHTC projects financed with tax-exempt bonds, which also preserve the existing affordable housing stock. Enhancing the basis of qualifying projects would increase the amount of LIHTC eligible projects could receive.

Designate Growth Zones

A variety of tax incentives are available under current law to foster the development of certain geographic areas, such as empowerment zones (EZs), enterprise zones, and the Gulf Opportunity Zone (GO Zone). Presently, there are 40 EZs—30 in urban areas and 10 in rural areas—which have been designated as such through a competitive process that has spanned three separate rounds in 1994, 1998, and 2002. Businesses located in an EZ may qualify for several tax benefits, including a 20% wage credit, an enhanced expensing allowance for qualified property placed in service within an EZ, and tax-exempt financing for certain qualified zone facilities. To be eligible for these benefits, a firm must generate at least 50% of its gross receipts from the active conduct of a qualified line of business within the zone, a substantial portion of its fixed assets must be located within the zone, and at least 35% of its employees must reside there.

---

[9] For more information about BABs, see CRS Report R40523, *Tax Credit Bonds: Overview and Analysis*, by Steven Maguire.

[10] Thomson-Reuters as provided by the Securities Industry and Financial Markets Association (SIFMA). Data available at http://www.sifma.org/research/statistics.aspx.

[11] For more information about the LIHTC program, see CRS Report RS22389, *An Introduction to the Design of the Low-Income Housing Tax Credit*, by Mark P. Keightley.

The GO Zone encompasses the area devastated by Hurricane Katrina in 2005 that President Bush declared a federal disaster area. Numerous tax incentives were established to facilitate the re-development of the zone, but most of them have expired. Four of the incentives are available through the end of 2011: (1) an increase in available tax-exempt bond financing, (2) an increase in the allocation of low-income housing tax credits, (3) an increase in the rehabilitation credit rate for structures located in the zone, and (4) full expensing for qualified property placed in service in the zone in 2011.

The President's budget proposes replacing this mix of tax incentives for regional economic development with a plan to designate 20 growth zones (14 in urban areas and 6 in rural areas), beginning on January 1, 2012. These designations, which would be chosen through a competitive process by the Secretary of Commerce in consultation with the Secretaries of Agriculture and Housing and Urban Development, would remain in effect from January 1, 2012, through December 31, 2016. A key consideration in the selection process would be an applicant's "competitiveness plan" and its need to attract investment and jobs. For a plan to succeed, it should clearly explain how its economic strategy would link the zone to regional drivers of economic growth. Two tax incentives would be available for businesses located in a growth zone: (1) a credit equal to 20% of the first $15,000 in wages paid to employees who reside in the zone; the credit drops to 10% for zone residents who are employed outside the zone, and (2) full expensing for qualified property placed in service in the zone.

Continue Certain Expiring Provisions Through Calendar Year 2012

The federal tax code contains numerous temporary provisions, many of which are routinely extended, but not always before they expire. A variety of temporary individual and business tax provisions have already expired or are due to expire on or before December 31, 2011. These include tax credits for the construction of energy-efficient new homes and the purchase of energy-efficient appliances; an optional deduction for state and local sales taxes; a deduction for qualified tuition and related expenses; an employment credit for native Americans; 15-year straight-line depreciation for qualified leasehold, restaurant, and retail store improvements; and the work opportunity tax credit.

The President's budget proposes to extend over 50 expired or soon-to-expire tax provisions through the end of 2012, at a five-year revenue cost of $20.5 billion. Four provisions account for 55% of the projected cost: incentives for alcohol fuels ($4.8 billion over five years), extension and modification of the IRC Section 25C credit for energy efficiency improvements to existing homes ($1.1 billion), optional deduction for state and local sales taxes ($2.3 billion), and the exception under sub-part F for income derived from active financing ($3.1 billion). For provisions due to expire at the end of 2011, the extensions would go into effect on January 1, 2012; for those that have already expired or will expire before the end of 2011, the extensions would be retroactive to the date of expiration.

Alternative Minimum Tax (AMT) Relief

The President's budget proposal would patch the Alternative Minimum Tax (AMT) for three years, for 2011 through 2013. The FY2012 budget would pay for this patch by reducing the value of certain tax expenditures through limiting itemized deductions. The budget also includes an alternative "PAYGO" baseline that goes farther than the explicit budget proposal.[12] The PAYGO baseline differs from current law by assuming that certain expiring tax provisions are extended. Under current law, the AMT will revert to the tax year 2000 parameters for the 2011 tax year. The PAYGO baseline in the FY2012 budget assumes the AMT is patched in 2011 and then permanently adjusted for inflation based on 2011 parameters. The result of this alternative PAYGO baseline is an underestimation of the cost in foregone tax collection.

The provision intended to pay for the three-year AMT patch is the limitation on itemized deductions for taxpayers in the highest income tax brackets. Many taxpayers in the 33% tax bracket and all the taxpayers in the 35% bracket would only be allowed to reduce taxable income by an amount equivalent to a taxpayer in the 28% tax bracket. For example, under existing law, a taxpayer in the 33% bracket with $20,000 of itemized deductions would reduce their tax liability by $6,600 ($20,000 multiplied by 33%). Under the FY2012 budget proposal, the same taxpayer would reduce their tax liability by $5,600 ($20,000 multiplied by 28%).

Other Revenue Changes and "Loophole Closers"

The President's budget proposes a range of other proposals that are aimed at reforming the taxation of financial institutions, insurance companies, and U.S. multinational businesses; eliminating tax preferences for fossil fuels; reducing the tax gap; and modifying the estate and gift tax. The Administration estimates that these proposals would increase revenues by $166.2 billion over 5 years and $356.5 billion over 10 years.

Reform Treatment of Financial Institutions and Products

The President's budget proposes four changes to the tax treatment of financial institutions and products. A proposed "financial crisis responsibility" fee would have the largest revenue effect. The fee would be imposed on U.S.-based financial institutions with assets greater than $50 billion and U.S. subsidiaries of international financial institutions with assets greater than $50 billion. The fee would be equal to 7.5 basis points (0.075%) of covered liabilities and would take effect in 2013.

The Administration's other three reform proposals have smaller revenue effects and are somewhat more complicated. One proposal would require corporations that agree to sell their stock at some point in the future in exchange for future compensation to recognize taxable interest income from transactions beginning in 2012. The objective is to create tax parity with corporations that must recognize taxable interest income when they agree to sell their stock now in exchange for future compensation.

Another proposal would require dealers in securities, equity options, commodities, and commodities derivatives to treat the income (or loss) from their dealer activities as ordinary income instead of as 60% long-term capital gain (or loss) and 40% short-term capital gain (or loss) as they currently do. The objective of this proposal is to create tax parity with dealers in other property whose income is treated as ordinary for tax purposes. The Administration's last

---

[12] The PAYGO baseline is intended to more accurately reflect the cost of tax proposals.

proposal would modify the definition of "control" to include indirect control relationships for purposes of IRC Section 249, which may disallow or limit the deduction for premiums paid to repurchase debt instruments.

Reinstate Superfund Taxes

Congress appropriates monies from the Superfund Trust Fund to finance the cleanup of contamination from hazardous substances, under the Superfund program administered by the Environmental Protection Agency (EPA).[13] Historically, dedicated industry taxes provided most of the revenues until the taxing authority expired at the end of 1995. These taxes consisted of three excise taxes (one for petroleum, one for certain chemical feedstocks, and one for imported substances made from those same chemicals) and a special environmental tax on corporate income. As the remaining revenues were expended over time, Congress increased the portion of general revenues to help compensate for the loss of the dedicated taxes. General revenues now constitute most, but not all, of the source of revenues for the trust fund. Cost recoveries collected from liable parties, fines and penalties assessed for violations of cleanup requirements, and interest on the unexpended balance of the trust fund continue to contribute monies that augment general revenues. Through EPA enforcement actions, sites with financially viable parties who are liable for the contamination also pay for the cleanup directly using their own funds. These private funds provide additional cleanup resources and help to reserve Superfund appropriations for sites at which the liable parties cannot afford to pay or cannot be found.

Whether to reinstate the dedicated industry taxes has been a long-standing issue since the expiration of the taxing authority at the end of 1995. The debate has involved numerous issues regarding whether the taxes ensure that polluters pay for the cleanup of contamination, or whether the taxes may place an unfair burden of the costs on certain parties who did not cause or contribute to contamination. The Administration proposes reinstating the three excise taxes and the environmental tax on corporate income at the rates that were in effect when the taxes expired at the end of 1995. As a result, an excise tax would be imposed on domestic crude oil and imported petroleum products at a rate of 9.7 cents a barrel; a second excise tax would be imposed on the production of chemical feedstocks at a rate that varies by individual chemical from 22 cents to $4.87 per ton; and an excise tax would be imposed on imported substances made from the same hazardous chemicals targeted by the second excise at the same rate that would have applied if those chemicals had been subject to the feedstocks tax. In addition, corporations would be subject to an environmental income tax equal to 0.12% of the amount by which a corporation's modified alternative minimum taxable income exceeds $2 million. Under the proposal, these taxes would be reinstated on January 1, 2012, and expire on December 31, 2021.

Increase the Oil Spill Liability Trust Fund Financing Rate by One Cent

Under current law, the revenue raised by an excise tax (imposed at a rate of eight cents a barrel through the end of 2016 and nine cents thereafter) on domestic crude oil production and imports

---

[13] For more information on the Superfund Trust Fund and the Superfund program, see CRS Report R41039, *Comprehensive Environmental Response, Compensation, and Liability Act: A Summary of Superfund Cleanup Authorities and Related Provisions of the Act*, by David M. Bearden.

of petroleum products is deposited in the Oil Spill Trust Fund (OSTF). Money in the fund is used to pay for the costs associated with the cleanup of oil spills and the economic damage they cause. The funds are also used to help pay for federal oil pollution and prevention and response programs. There is some concern that the balance in the fund may be insufficient to address the costs associated with oil spills similar in magnitude to the Deepwater Horizon spill in 2010.

The Administration proposes raising the rate of the OSTF tax to nine cents a barrel starting January 1, 2012, and then to 10 cents a barrel starting January 1, 2017.

Make the Unemployment Insurance Tax Permanent

Under the Federal Unemployment Tax Act (FUTA), employers are assessed a 6.2% payroll tax on the first $7,000 in wages paid to each employee. This rate includes a 0.2% temporary surtax that Congress first established in 1976 and has extended several times; the current surtax is due to expire on June 30, 2011. Revenue from the tax funds a portion of the unemployment benefits system that is jointly managed by the federal and state governments.

States also impose an unemployment tax on employers. But employers in states that satisfy certain federal requirements may claim a credit for state unemployment taxes equal to as much as 5.4% of the first $7,000 in wages paid to an employee. As a result, the minimum net federal FUTA rate is 0.8%, which consists of a 0.6% permanent tax rate and the temporary surtax rate of 0.2%.

The President's budget proposes to permanently extend the 0.2% surtax, as of the date of enactment.

Repeal Last-In, First-Out (LIFO) Method of Accounting for Inventories

Many companies hold inventories of inputs and products for sale. They cannot deduct the cost of inventory items when purchased, because the transactions involve an exchange of cash for assets of equal value. So to compute profits, companies deduct the cost of inventory against the sale of goods. Since identical goods moving out of inventory can have different acquisition costs, companies rely on certain accounting conventions to account for the cost of goods sold.

Most companies use the first-in, first-out method (FIFO) of accounting for the cost of inventory, which assumes that the goods bought first are also the ones sold first. Companies have the option of using the last-in, first-out method (LIFO), which assumes that the goods first purchased make up a company's inventory at the close of the business year. During a period of rising prices, LIFO assigns higher costs to goods sold, reducing current income and the value of year-end inventory. As a result, LIFO can create a tax benefit by allowing taxpayers that hold inventories whose costs are increasing over time to defer taxation of a portion of their income. Use of the LIFO method is not permitted under International Financial Reporting Standards.

The Administration proposes to disallow the use of the LIFO method for federal income tax purposes. Under the proposal, taxpayers that currently use this method would be required to convert their beginning LIFO inventory to its FIFO value in the first tax year starting after December 31, 2012. The resulting rise in gross income would be taken into account ratably over the following 10 years.

Repeal the Gain Limitation for Dividends Received in Reorganization Exchanges

When a shareholder receives both stock and non-stock considerations in a reorganization under IRC Section 368, IRC Section 356 applies to any gains from the transaction. Under IRC Section 356, any gain realized by a taxpayer on an exchange of stock in a target company for stock in an acquiring company and cash (or boot) is recognized to the extent of the cash received (the so-called boot-within-a-gain limitation). In addition, the recognized gain is taxed as a dividend if the exchange is equivalent to the distribution of a dividend and the acquiring company has sufficient earnings and profits; the remainder of the recognized gain is considered a long-term capital gain. No loss is recognized on the exchange. These rules mean that the shareholder exchanging the stock has a taxable income from the transaction that is equal to the lesser of the cash received or the total gain realized on the exchange, and this income is either capital gain or dividend income, depending on the facts and circumstances.

The Administration is asking Congress to repeal the boot-within-a-gain limitation when an exchange of stock under a Section 368 reorganization is equivalent to the distribution of a dividend. In seeking the change, the Administration wants to make the tax treatment of dividends more uniform and prevent the repatriation of the profits held by foreign subsidiaries of U.S. corporations with minimal taxation through reorganizations. The proposal would go into effect on January 1, 2012.

Reform U.S. International Tax System

The tax proposals made in the FY2012 budget request reflect the Administration's priorities for international tax reform. Several proposals for repeal of certain incentives would raise substantial revenue. Proponents argue that these measures will help close the tax gap. Opponents have expressed concerns over their effect on economic growth and competitiveness.[14] Taken together, the Administration estimates that they will raise an additional $65.0 billion over 5 years and $129.2 over 10 years.

Defer Deduction of Expenses Related to Deferred Income

U.S. parent firms can deduct expenses of foreign subsidiaries, such as interest, while not recognizing income from those foreign subsidiaries that is not repatriated (not paid to the parent as dividends).[15] U.S. parents can thus benefit from deductions, while not including earnings in income. The President's budget proposal would defer the deduction of a portion of these costs until the income is repatriated. This proposal would be effective beginning in 2012.

---

[14] For more on the economics related to many of the reform proposals, see CRS Report R40623, *Tax Havens: International Tax Avoidance and Evasion*, by Jane G. Gravelle.

[15] For detailed information, see CRS Report RL32749, *U.S. Taxation of Overseas Investment and Income: Background and Issues*, by Donald J. Marples.

Reform Foreign Tax Credit

U.S. firms with operations abroad are allowed a tax credit against their U.S. income tax liability for foreign taxes paid on foreign income currently subject to tax.[16] Foreign tax credits may be claimed on an "overall" basis, so that income and tax credits from all countries are combined. As a result, "cross-crediting," where credits paid in excess of U.S. tax in one country may be used to offset U.S. tax in a country where the foreign tax is lower than the U.S. tax, may occur. By applying excess credits generated in a high tax country to earnings repatriated from a low tax country, firms can avoid most U.S. tax.

Under the President's proposal, a U.S. firm would be required to determine its deemed paid foreign tax credit on a consolidated basis based on the aggregate foreign taxes and earnings and profits of all of the foreign subsidiaries with respect to which the U.S. taxpayer can claim a deemed paid foreign tax. This proposal would be effective beginning in 2012.

Tax Currently Excess Returns Associated with Transfers of Intangibles Offshore

Transactions between related parties, in particular transfers to low-taxed affiliates, can generate significant tax savings for U.S.-based multinational firms. The Administration's FY2012 budget proposal would provide that any excess income generated by such a transfer be included in subpart F income (subpart F income refers to income earned by foreign affiliates of majority owned U.S. firms). Excess income is defined as the excess of gross income beyond what the properly apportioned and allocated costs to generate this income would merit. The proposal would be effective for transactions beginning January 1, 2012.

Limit Shifting of Income Through Intangible Property Transfers

The President's budget proposes clarifying the definition of intangible property and the allocation of income and deductions among the parties involved. Taxpayers may sell, lease, or otherwise transfer intangible property to foreign corporations. If the appropriate royalty or other arms-length payment for use of the property is not made, profits can be artificially shifted to low tax jurisdictions. The President's proposes clarifying some regulations to try to reduce this scope of this shifting. The proposal would be effective for transactions beginning January 1, 2012.

Disallow the Deduction for Excess Non-Taxed Reinsurance Premiums Paid to Affiliates

U.S. insurance companies pay for reinsurance through premiums paid to a reinsurer. The premium payments are deductible expenses for the U.S insurance company. If the payment is in the form of income producing asset, the income generated by the asset is taxable if the reinsurer is a U.S. company. If, however, the reinsurer is a foreign company, this income would avoid U.S. income taxes. For reinsurance premiums paid to a foreign reinsurer, the U.S. levies an excise tax of 1% on the premium paid.

---

[16] For detailed information, see CRS Report RL32749, *U.S. Taxation of Overseas Investment and Income: Background and Issues*, by Donald J. Marples.

The 1% excise tax is still significantly less than the income tax that would be paid if the reinsurer were a U.S. company. The Administration's FY2012 budget proposal would deny the deduction for reinsurance premium payments if paid to a foreign reinsurer. The provision would also exclude from the U.S. insurance company's income any reinsurance recovered from reinsurance paid for with non-deductible premiums. The proposal would be effective beginning January 1, 2012.

Limit Earnings Stripping by Expatriated Entities

A number of high profile U.S. based companies have recently realized tax savings by nominally becoming foreign based companies through a process known as inversion or expatriation.[17] After completing the inversion, the companies new "parent" is technically located outside the United States, while the old "parent" is a subsidiary operating within the United States. The new foreign based parent may then loan money to its U.S. subsidiary. The U.S. subsidiary is able to lower its U.S. tax liability by deducting the interest payments on the loan. The President's budget proposes to limit this practice, known as earnings stripping, by disallowing the deduction for interest on loans made within an inverted entity in instances where interest deductions are large relative to income. The proposal would be effective beginning January 1, 2012.

Modify Tax Rules for Dual Capacity Taxpayers

U.S. taxpayers are allowed a tax credit against their U.S. income tax liability for foreign taxes paid. The credit, known as the foreign tax credit, is intended to alleviate the double taxation of income. In some instances, foreign taxes that are paid are in exchange for a direct economic benefit provided by the foreign government. An example are payments that are effectively royalty for the extraction of oil and gas. Taxpayers involved in a such an exchange are referred to as dual capacity taxpayers, and are generally disallowed the foreign tax credit by U.S. regulations. The President's budget proposes to tighten the foreign tax credit rules that apply to dual capacity earners.

Reform Treatment of Insurance Companies and Products

The President budget proposes to modify the taxation of insurance companies and selected insurance products through three specific proposals. Taken together, the Administration estimates that they will raise an additional $3.7 billion over 5 years and $14.1 over 10 years.

Modify Rules that Apply to the Sales of Life Insurance Contracts

Under current law, an exclusion from Federal income tax is provided for amounts received from a life insurance contract paid by reason of the death of the insured. If the rights to the proceeds of the contract are sold prior to the insured's death (a life settlement transaction), this exclusion is limited and the transaction may be taxable. The President's budget proposes to expand information reporting for these transactions. The proposal is likely directed at reducing the

---

[17] For detailed information, see CRS Report RL31444, *Firms That Incorporate Abroad for Tax Purposes: Corporate "Inversions" and "Expatriation,"* by Donald J. Marples.

portion of the tax gap associated with non reporting or under reporting of this income. The proposal would take effect for tax years beginning in 2012.

Modify Dividends-Received Deduction for Life Insurance Company Separate Accounts

The President's budget proposes to simplify the regime which restricts the ability of insurance companies to fund tax deductible reserve increases with tax preferred income. This provision may be attempting to reduce the tax differences between life insurance companies and other companies, which, generally, can not engage in this type of tax arbitrage. The proposal would take effect for tax years beginning in 2012.

Expand Pro-Rate Interest Expense Disallowance for Corporate-Owned Life Insurance (COLI)

The President's budget proposes to eliminate the exception under the pro rata interest deduction disallowance rule for employees, officers and directors—for all but 20-percent owners. As with the prior provision, this provision may be attempting to restrict a tax arbitrage opportunity. The proposal would take effect for tax years beginning in 2012.

Eliminate Fossil-Fuel Tax Preferences

President Obama agreed at the G-20 Summit in Pittsburgh in September 2009 to phase out fossil-fuel subsidies. The Leaders' Statement from the Pittsburgh Summit noted "Inefficient fossil fuel subsidies encourage wasteful consumption, reduce our energy security, impede investment in clean energy sources and undermine efforts to deal with the threat of climate change."[18] The President's FY2012 budget proposes to eliminate tax preferences for coal and oil and gas. The Administration estimates elimination of the fossil-fuel tax preferences will raise an additional $24.0 billion over 5 years and $46.2 over 10 years.

Eliminate Coal Preferences

Expensing of Exploration and Development Costs

Special rules allow taxpayers to expense costs associated with identifying and locating ore or mineral deposits, including coal. Generally, costs that benefit future periods must be capitalized and recovered over time. Allowing coal-related exploration and development costs to be expensed encourages investment in coal production. The FY2012 budget proposes to change the tax treatment of coal-related exploration and development costs, so that such costs are capitalized and deducted over time according to generally applicable rules. Such a change would make cost recovery for coal investments similar to cost recovery in other industries. This proposal would be effective beginning December 31, 2011.

---

[18] The Pittsburgh Summit, "Leaders' Statement: The Pittsburgh Summit," press release, September 25, 2009, at http://www.pittsburghsummit.gov/documents/organization/129853.pdf.

Percentage Depletion for Hard Mineral Fossil Fuels

Firms that extract coal and other hard-mineral fossil fuels are permitted a deduction to recover their capital investment in a mineral reserve, which depreciates due to the physical and economic depletion or exhaustion as the mineral is recovered. Depletion, like depreciation, is a form of capital recovery. One method for computing the deduction is the percentage depletion.[19] Under percentage depletion, the deduction for recovery of capital investment is a fixed percentage of the "gross income"—namely, revenue—from the sale of the mineral. Typically, despite limitations, total deductions under this method exceed the capital invested to acquire and develop the reserve. By reducing tax rates, percentage depletion encourages investment in coal and other hard-mineral fossil fuels. The FY2012 budget proposes to eliminate percentage depletion, allowing fossil-fuel producers to instead claim cost depletion. This proposal would be effective beginning December 31, 2011.

Capital Gains Treatment for Royalties

Royalties from certain dispositions of coal are treated as long-term capital gains, and thereby taxed at a reduced rate. Generally, royalties are taxed at ordinary rates. The favorable capital gains treatment of coal royalties encourages investment in coal. The FY2012 budget proposes eliminating the capital gains treatment of coal royalties. This proposal would be effective beginning December 31, 2011.

Domestic Manufacturing Deduction for Coal and other Hard-Mineral Fossil Fuels

A deduction is allowed with respect to income attributable to domestic production activities (IRC Section 199). The deduction is generally equal to 9% of the lesser of qualified production activities income or taxable income. Under current law, qualified income includes income generated from the sale, exchange, or disposition of coal or other hard-mineral fossil fuels. The Section 199 deduction reduces the effective tax rate for qualified activities, encouraging investment in such activities. The FY2012 budget proposes to exclude from the definition of qualified activities the sale, exchange, or disposition of coal and other hard-mineral fossil fuels. This proposal would be effective beginning December 31, 2011.

Eliminate Oil and Gas Preferences

Enhanced Oil Recovery Credit

A 15% credit is available for qualifying enhanced oil recovery (EOR) costs. Qualifying EOR costs include the costs of tangible equipment; intangible drilling and development costs; and deductible tertiary injectant costs. The credit is phased out once the price of oil exceeds the legislatively determined reference price. In recent years, the price of oil has been high enough such that the EOR credit has been fully phased out. The FY2012 budget proposes to repeal the EOR credit. This proposal would be effective beginning December 31, 2011.

---

[19] The second method is cost depletion.

Credit for Oil and Gas Produced from Marginal Wells

Production of crude oil and natural gas from marginal wells are eligible for a tax credit. A marginal well is defined under IRC Section 45I(c)(3). The maximum credit amount is $3 per barrel of qualified oil production and $0.50 per 1,000 cubic feet of qualified gas production. The credit is phased out once the price of oil exceeds the legislatively determined reference price. In recent years, the price of oil has been high enough such that the EOR credit has been fully phased out. The FY2012 budget proposes to repeal the credit for production from marginal wells. This proposal would be effective beginning December 31, 2011.

Expensing of Intangible Drilling Costs

Intangible drilling costs (IDCs) are expenditures paid by the firms engaged in the exploration and development of oil, gas, or geothermal properties for fuel, labor, repairs to drilling equipment, materials, hauling, and supplies. Under current law, IDCs may be partially or fully expensed (deducted in the year they are incurred) rather than capitalized (recovered over time through depletion or depreciation). The option to expense IDCs applies to domestic properties, which include certain off-shore wells (essentially those within the exclusive economic zone of the United States), generally including offshore platforms. The FY2012 budget proposes eliminating the expensing allowance for IDCs. Instead, IDCs would be capitalized and the costs recovered over time. This proposal would be effective beginning December 31, 2011.

Deduction for Tertiary Injectants

Current law allows taxpayers to claim a deduction for the cost of qualifying tertiary injectants. Tertiary injectants are used as part of a tertiary recovery method to increase the recovery of crude oil. The FY2012 budget proposes to eliminate the deduction for tertiary injectants. This proposal would be effective beginning December 31, 2011.

Exception to Passive Loss Limitations for Working Interests in Oil and Natural Gas Properties

Losses by a taxpayer with a passive ownership interest in a business are generally not deductible against other forms of income. Unused passive losses may be carried forward to offset passive income in the future. In general, a passive interest is one in which the taxpayer does not materially participate in the business's operation. One exception is the ownership of a working interest in an oil or natural gas property. The owner of a working interest may deduct losses from such interest against other (non-passive) income. The FY2012 budget proposes to eliminate the exception to passive loss limitations for working interests in oil and natural gas property. This proposal would be effective beginning December 31, 2011.

Percentage Depletion for Oil and Natural Gas

Firms that extract oil, gas, or other minerals are permitted a deduction to recover their capital investment in a mineral reserve, which depreciates due to the physical and economic depletion or exhaustion as the mineral is recovered. Depletion, like depreciation, is a form of capital recovery.

One method for computing the deduction is the percentage depletion.[20] Under percentage depletion, the deduction for recovery of capital investment is a fixed percentage of the "gross income"—namely, revenue—from the sale of the mineral. Typically, despite limitations, total deductions under this method exceed the capital invested to acquire and develop the reserve. The FY2012 budget proposes to eliminate percentage depletion, allowing oil and gas producers to instead claim cost depletion. This proposal would be effective beginning December 31, 2011.

Domestic Manufacturing Deduction for Oil and Natural Gas Companies

A deduction is allowed with respect to income attributable to domestic production activities (IRC § 199). The deduction is generally equal to 9% of the lesser of qualified production activities income or taxable income. The deduction for income from oil and gas properties is limited to 6%. Under current law, qualified income includes income generated from the sale, exchange, or disposition of oil, natural gas, or primary products thereof. The Section 199 deduction reduces the effective tax rate for qualified activities, encouraging investment in such activities. The FY2012 budget proposes to exclude from the definition of qualified activities the sale, exchange, or disposition of oil, natural gas, or primary products thereof. This proposal would be effective beginning December 31, 2011.

Increase Geological and Geophysical Amortization Period for Independent Producers

The amortization period for geological and geophysical expenditures for independent oil and gas producers is two years and seven years for integrated oil and gas producers. Geological and geophysical expenditures are costs associated with obtaining and accumulating data on mineral properties. A reduced amortization period allows these costs to be recovered over a shorter period of time, encouraging investment. The FY2012 budget proposes to increase the amortization period for geological and geophysical expenditures for independent oil and gas producers from two to seven years. This proposal would be effective beginning December 31, 2011.

Tax Carried (Profits) Interest as Ordinary Income

A partnership does not pay income taxes, instead gains and losses flow through to the partners who include it on their income tax returns. The income from the partnership is often taxed as capital gains or qualified dividends at reduced tax rates (i.e., 15%). Some partners receive partnership interests in exchange for contributions of capital (that is, investments) and are limited partners; some partners receive partnership interests in exchange for services (carried interests) and these are general partners who actively manage the partnership. The Administration is proposing to designate a general partner's share of partnership income that is not attributable to invested capital as ordinary income, which would be taxed at the higher individual income tax rates rather than at the reduced capital gains tax rate. In addition, this share of income would be subject to self-employment taxes. The Administration projects this tax change will increase tax revenues by $10.1 billion over 5 years and $14.8 billion over 10 years.

---

[20] The second method is cost depletion.

Deny Deduction for Punitive Damages

Under certain circumstances, punitive damages paid a taxpayer can be deducted. The deduction is allowed for damages paid as ordinary and necessary expenses in carrying on a business. The Administration has proposed not allowing a deduction for punitive damages paid, arguing the deduction undermines the role that damages play in discouraging and penalizing undesirable activities. This proposal is projected to increase tax revenues by $127 million over 5 years and $312 million over 10 years.

Repeal Lower-of-Cost-or-Market Inventory Accounting Method

A taxpayer maintaining inventories (e.g., a business holding unsold goods) may use a variety of methods to determine the end of accounting period cost of the inventories. One method is the lower-of-cost-or-market (LCM) method, and it is argued this method understates taxable income. The method basically allows losses on inventory to be recognized and deducted against income for tax purposed without an actual transaction taking place (an unrealized loss), but unrealized gains are not recognized and added to income. The Administration argues that this asymmetric treatment of inventory valuation is unwarranted and proposes to prohibit the use of the LCM method. This proposal is projected to increase tax revenues by $5.5 billion over 5 years and $8.1 billion over 10 years.

Simplify the Tax Code

The Administration has proposed 11 relatively minor items to simplify the tax code. These items mostly reduce the burden of administering some tax provisions (and reducing tax avoidance) or reduce the complexity of certain provisions for taxpayers. The items would affect tax provisions dealing with the plug-in electric-drive motor vehicle credit, individual retirement accounts, employee stock option plans, partnerships, publicly-traded REITs, and private foundations. In addition, three items would reduce the complexity and compliance burdens of tax-exempt bonds on State and local governments. These items are projected to increase tax revenues by $148 million over 5 years and decrease tax revenues by $407 million over 10 years.

Reduce The Tax Gap and Make Reforms

The President's budget contains a number of proposals aimed at reducing the tax gap and making other reforms. The proposals are intended to expand information reporting, improve tax compliance, strengthen tax administration, and modify the estate and gift tax. The proposed changes are estimated to increase tax revenues by $7.8 billion over 5 years and $20.9 billion over 10 years.

Expand Information Reporting

The Internal Revenue Service (IRS) has found that third-party information reporting reduces tax evasion because the IRS can match data on the information reporting forms with data reported by taxpayers. Over the years, the number of information reporting forms has greatly increased. Better information reporting, however, imposes higher compliance costs on taxpayers, reduces the privacy of taxpayers, and raises IRS administrative costs.

Repeal and Modify Information Reporting on Payments to Corporations and Payments for Property

The Patient Protection and Affordable Care Act (P.L. 111-148) expanded the information reporting requirement to include payments by taxpayers to a corporation (except a tax-exempt corporation) and payments for property. The proposal would repeal the information reporting requirement in P.L. 111-148 because the number and complexity of corporate taxpayers have increased, some taxpayers would have compliance issues, and some small businesses would have an undue compliance burden.

The proposal would require businesses to file an information return for payments for services to a corporation (except a tax-exempt corporation). Information returns would not be required for payments for property. This reduced reporting requirement would have a net effect of lowering federal revenue. The proposal would be effective for payments made after December 31, 2011.

Require Information Reporting for Private Separate Accounts of Life Insurance Companies

Policyholders of life insurance are not eligible for tax-free or tax-deferred income if they have control—through a life insurance company—over investments in a separate account to the degree that the policyholder, and not the insurance company, is considered the owner of the investments. In some cases, private separate accounts are being used to avoid income tax that would be due if the assets were held directly. The proposal would require life insurance companies to report information to the IRS, for each contract whose cash value is partially or wholly invested in a private separate account for any portion of the taxable year and represents at least 10% of the value of the account. The proposal would be effective for taxable years beginning after December 31, 2011.

Require a Certified Taxpayer Identification Number (TIN) from Contractors and Allow Certain Withholding

Currently, the IRS does not have accurate taxpayer identifying information on contractors, because of inadequate information reporting. The proposal would require a contractor receiving payments of $600 or more in a calendar year from a particular business to furnish to the business the contractor's certified TIN. A business would be required to verify the contractor's TIN with the IRS, which would be authorized to disclose, solely for this purpose, whether the certified TIN-name combination matches IRS records. If a contractor failed to furnish an accurate certified TIN, the business would be required to withhold a flat-rate percentage of gross payments. The proposal would be effective for payments made to contractors after December 31, 2011.

Improve Compliance by Businesses

Require Greater Electronic Filing of Returns

Currently, those corporations, partnerships, and tax-exempt organizations, that have assets of $10 million or more and file annually more than 250 returns, are required to file Schedule M-3 electronically. Generally, compliance increases when taxpayers are required to provide better information to the IRS in usable form. Large organizations with assets of $10 million or more generally maintain financial records in electronic form. The proposal would require all corporations and partnerships that must file Schedule M-3 to file their income tax returns electronically. The proposal would be effective for taxable years ending after December 31, 2011.

Authorize the Department of the Treasury to Require Additional Information to Be Included in Electronically Filed Form 5500 Annual Reports

Currently sponsors of a funded plan of deferred compensation (or the administrator of the plan) and certain pension and welfare benefit plans (under ERISA) are required to file an annual report (Form 5500 and attachments) disclosing certain information to the Department of Labor (DOL). The proposal would provide the IRS with the authority to require that the electronically filed annual reports include information that is relevant only to employee benefit plan tax requirements. This additional electronic filing of information will assist the IRS in improving tax compliance. The proposal would be effective for plan years beginning after December 31, 2011.

Implement Standards Clarifying When Employee Leasing Companies Can Be Held Liable for Their Clients' Federal Employment Taxes

Employee leasing is the practice of contracting with an outside business to handle certain administrative, personnel, and payroll matters for a taxpayer's employees. Employee leasing companies typically prepare and file employment tax returns for their clients using the leasing company's name and employer identification number, often taking the position that the leasing company is the statutory or common law employer of their clients' workers. The proposal would set forth standards for holding employee leasing companies jointly liable with their clients for federal employment taxes. The proposal would also provide standards for holding employee leasing companies solely liable for such taxes if they meet specified requirements. The provision would be effective for employment tax returns required to be filed with respect to wages paid after December 31, 2011.

Increase Certainty With Respect to Worker Classification

Under current tax law, workers must be classified into one of two mutually exclusive categories: employees or self-employed (sometimes referred to as independent contractors). A business owner must withhold and remit income taxes, Social Security and Medicare taxes; and pay unemployment taxes on wages paid to an employee. In contrast, a business owner does not have to withhold and remit taxes or pay unemployment taxes on payments to independent contractors.

Worker classification generally is based on a common-law test for determining whether an employment relationship exists. Under common-law rules, a worker is an employee if the employer can control what the worker does and how the worker does it. Currently, the IRS states that three categories of common-law rules provide evidence of the degree of control and independence: behavior, financial, and type of relationship. The definition of "employee" has been affected by IRC Section 530 "Safe Harbor Rules," which were enacted in the Revenue Act of 1978 (P.L. 95-600). If an employer qualifies for the safe harbor rules, then generally the employer is allowed to treat a worker as not being an employee for employment tax purposes, regardless of the individual's actual status under the common-law test.

Employers are more likely to withhold and submit taxes than independent contractors are to voluntarily pay their tax liabilities, consequently the misclassification of employees as independent contractors contributes to the tax gap.

The proposal would permit the IRS to require prospective reclassification of workers who are currently misclassified and whose reclassification has been prohibited under current law. The Department of the Treasury and the IRS also would be permitted to issue generally applicable guidance on the proper classification of workers under common law standards. This would enable service recipients to properly classify workers with much less concern about future IRS examinations. Treasury and the IRS would be directed to issue guidance interpreting common law in a neutral manner recognizing that many workers are, in fact, not employees.

The proposal would be effective upon enactment, but prospective reclassification of those covered by current special provision would not be effective until the first calendar year beginning at least one year after date of enactment. The transition period could be up to two years for independent contractors with existing written contracts establishing their status.

Repeal Special Estimated Tax Payment Provision for Certain Insurance Companies

Under current law, an insurance company uses reserve accounting to compute losses incurred. That is, losses incurred for the taxable year includes losses paid during the taxable year (net of salvage and reinsurance recovered), plus or minus the increase or decrease in discounted unpaid losses during the year. An adjustment is also made for the change in discounted estimated salvage and reinsurance recoverable. Unpaid losses are determined on a discounted basis to account for the time that may elapse between an insured loss event and the payment or other resolution of the claim. Taxpayers may, however, elect under IRC Section 847 to take an additional deduction equal to the difference between the amount of their reserves computed on a discounted basis and the amount computed on an undiscounted basis.

Although this provision is revenue neutral, it imposes a substantial recordkeeping burden on both taxpayers and the IRS. The proposal would repeal IRC Section 847, and the entire balance of any existing special loss discount account would be included in gross income.

In lieu of immediate inclusion in gross income for the first taxable year beginning after December 31, 2011, taxpayers would be permitted to elect to include the balance of any existing special loss discount account in gross income ratable over a four taxable year period, beginning with the first taxable year beginning after December 31, 2011.

Repeal Special Rules Modifying the Amount of Estimated Tax Payments by Corporations

Under IRC Section 6655, corporations generally are required to pay their income tax liability for a taxable year in quarterly estimated payments. A number of acts have modified this standard rules as to the amount due by "large corporations" for a particular quarter. The frequent changes to the corporate estimated tax payment schedule do not generally increase a corporation's income tax liability for a particular taxable year. However, the frequency of such changes operates to increase uncertainty within the corporate tax system. The proposal would repeal all legislative acts that cause the amount and timing of corporate estimated payments to differ from the rules described under Section 6655. The proposal would be effective for taxable years beginning after December 31, 2011.

Strengthen Tax Administration

Revise Offer-in-Compromise Application Rules

Current law provides that the IRS may compromise any civil or criminal case arising under the internal revenue laws prior to a reference to the Department of Justice for prosecuting or defense. In 2006, a new provision was enacted to require taxpayers to make certain nonrefundable payments with an initial offer-in-compromise of a tax case. Requiring nonrefundable payments with an offer-in-compromise may substantially reduce access to the offer-in-compromise program. The proposal would eliminate the requirements that an initial offer-in-compromise include a nonrefundable payment of any portion of the taxpayer's offer. The proposal would be effective for offers-in-compromise submitted after the date of enactment.

Expand Internal Revenue Service Access to Information in the National Directory of New Hires for Tax Administration Purposes

Under current law, the Office of Child Support Enforcement of the Department of Health and Human Services maintains the National Directory of New Hires (NDNH), which is a database that contains data from Form W-4 for newly-hired employees, quarterly wage data from state workforce and federal agencies for all employees, and unemployment insurance data from state workforce agencies for all individuals who have applied for or received unemployment benefits. Under current provisions of the Social Security Act, the IRS may obtain data from the NDNH, but only for the purpose of administering the earned income tax credit (EITC) and verifying employment reported on a tax return. Employment data are useful to the IRS in administering a wide range of tax provisions beyond the EITC. The proposal would amend the Social Security Act to expand IRS access to NDNH data for general tax administration purposes. The proposal would be effective upon enactment.

Make Repeated Willful Failure to File a Tax Return a Felony

Current law provides that willful failure to file a tax return is a misdemeanor. A taxpayer who fails to file returns for multiple years commits a separate misdemeanor offense for each year. Increased criminal penalties would help to deter multiple willful failures to file tax returns. The proposal would provide that any person who willfully fails to file tax returns in any three years within any five consecutive year period, if the aggregated tax liability for such period is at least $50,000, would classify such failure as a felony. The proposal would be effective for returns required to be filed after December 31, 2011.

Facilitate Tax Compliance with Local Jurisdictions

Although federal tax returns and return information (FTI) generally are confidential, the IRS and the Treasury Department may share FTI with states as well as certain local government entities that are treated as states for this purpose. Generally, the purpose of information sharing is to facilitate tax administration. Indian Tribal Governments (ITGs) are not treated as states for purposes of information sharing. IRS and Treasury compliance activity, especially with respect to alcohol, tobacco, and fuel excise taxes, may necessitate information sharing with ITGs. For purposes of information sharing, the proposal would treat as states those ITGs that impose alcohol, tobacco, or fuel excise, or income, or wage taxes, to the extent necessary for ITG tax administration. The proposal would be effective for disclosures made after enactment.

Extend Statute of Limitations Where State Adjustment Affects Federal Tax Liability

In general, additional federal tax liabilities in the form of tax, interest, penalties and additions to tax must be assessed by the IRS within three years after the date a return is filed. The general statute of limitations serves as a barrier to the effective use by the IRS of state and local tax adjustment reports when the reports are provided by the state or local revenue agency to the IRS with little time remaining for assessments to be made at the federal level. The proposal would create an additional exception to the general three-year statute of limitations for assessment of federal tax liability resulting from adjustments to state or local tax liability. The proposal would be effective for returns required to be filed after December 31, 2011.

Improve Investigative Disclosure Statute

Generally, tax return information is confidential, unless a specific exception in the Code applies. In the case of tax administration, the Code permits Treasury and IRS officers and employees to disclose return information to the extent necessary to obtain information not otherwise reasonably available, in the course of an audit or investigation, as prescribed by regulation. Treasury regulations effective since 2003 state that the term "necessary" in this context does not mean essential or indispensable, but rather appropriate and helpful in obtaining the information sought. The proposal would clarify the taxpayer privacy law by stating that the law does not prohibit Treasury and IRS officers and employees from identifying themselves, their organizational affiliation, and the nature and subject of an investigation, when contacting third parties in connection with a civil or criminal tax investigation. The proposal would be effective for disclosures make after enactment.

Require Taxpayers Who Prepare Their returns Electronically but File Their Returns on Paper to Print Their Returns with a 2-D Bar Code

Taxpayers can prepare their tax returns electronically and, instead of filing their returns electronically, may print out a paper copy and file the return on paper by mailing it to the IRS. The proposal would require all taxpayers who prepare their tax returns electronically but print their returns and file them on paper to print their returns with a 2-D bar code that can be scanned by the IRS to convert the paper return into an electronic format. The proposal would be effective for tax returns filed after December 31, 2011.

Require Prisons Located in the United States to Provide Information to the Internal Revenue Service

The IRS is unable to cross reference tax returns received with a list of prison inmates to determine whether inmates are claiming tax benefits to which they are not entitled. The IRS has become aware that some incarcerated individuals are claiming tax benefits to which they may not be entitled. The proposal would require all prisons located in the United States to submit to the

IRS, by December 1 of each year, a list of names and validated Social Security numbers of all inmates serving sentences of one year or more. The proposal would be effective upon enactment.

Allow the Internal Revenue Service (IRS) to Absorb Credit and Debit Card Processing Fees for Certain Tax Payments

IRC Section 6311 permits the IRS to receive payment of taxes by any commercially acceptable means that the Secretary deems appropriate. When taxpayers agree to make additional payments during in telephone consultations with IRS agents, it is inefficient for both taxpayers and the IRS to require taxpayers to contact a third party service provider to make credit and debit card payments. The proposal would amend Section 6311(d) to allow the IRS to accept credit or debit card payments directly from taxpayers and to absorb the credit and debit card processing fees for certain tax payments, without charging a separate processing fee to the taxpayer. The proposal would be effective for payments make after the date of enactment.

Expand Penalties

Impose a Penalty on Failure to Comply with Electronic Filing Requirements

Certain corporations and tax-exempt organizations (including certain charitable trusts and private foundations) are required to file their returns electronically. Although there are additions to tax for the failure to file returns, there is no specific penalty for a failure to comply with a requirement to file electronically. The proposal would establish an assessable penalty for a failure to comply with a requirement of electronic format for a return that is filed. The proposal would be effective for returns required to be electronically filed after December 31, 2011.

Increase Penalty Imposed on Paid Preparers who Fail to Comply with Earned Income Tax Credit (EITC) Due Diligence Requirements

IRC Section 6695(g) imposes a $100 penalty on tax return preparers who fail to comply with the due diligence requirements imposed by regulations with respect to determining eligibility for, or the amount of, the EITC for each such failure. The IRS estimates that as many as a quarter of EITC claims are made in error. The proposal would increase the Section 6695(g) penalty from $100 to $500. The proposal would be effective for returns required to be filed after December 31, 2011.

Estate Tax

The President's budget proposal uses a policy baseline that would return the estate and gift tax parameters to those in place for the 2009 tax year for decedents in 2013 and beyond.[21] Specifically, under the alternative policy baseline, in 2013, the exemption amount would be $3.5 million. For 2011 and 2012, under P.L. 111-312, the exemption amount is $5 million with spouses allowed to transfer any unused exemption amount to the surviving spouse, creating the equivalent

---

[21] Under current law the estate tax reverts to the pre-2001-2003 tax cuts level of $1 million in 2013. For budget scoring purposes, it is against this baseline that the cost of the provision is measured.

of a $10 million exemption. The spousal transfer is typically referred to as portability. The budget proposes making the portability provision described above permanent. Thus, under the alternative policy baseline, the $3.5 exemption amount would become the equivalent of a $7 million exemption for married decedents.[22]

In addition to extending the portability option, the FY2012 budget includes additional modifications to estate taxes. First is a provision that would require inheritors to use the same basis (or value) for transferred assets from an estate when calculating future income tax liability. A second provision would make it more difficult to reduce the valuation of a transferred asset. Under current law, the value jointly held assets that include restrictions on resale can be reduced because the estate would not receive full market value with the restrictions. The budget proposal would identify certain restrictions that are under family control and that can be easily removed after death. These "soft" restrictions would be disregarded when determining valuation discounts.

Two more provisions are much more complicated, but are intended to close estate tax loopholes. The first would limit the value of so-called grantor annuity trusts (GRATs) and the second would modify the rules covering generation skipping taxes (GSTs) to make it more difficult to avoid estate taxes through multigenerational trust arrangements. These provisions are in response to popular tax planning techniques intended to reduce estate tax liability.

Cost Estimates

The Administration has estimated the cost of the President's FY2012 budget proposals. **Table 1** presents the 5- and 10-year estimates.

Table 1. The Administration's Cost Estimates for the President's FY2012 Budget Proposals

(all figures are in millions of dollars)

Provision	2012-2016	2012-2021
Tax Cuts For Families And Individuals	-91,928	-253,563
Expand earned income credit	-4,414	-12,313
Expand child and dependent care tax credit	-4,452	-9,605
Automatic enrollment in IRAs, employer enrollment tax credit, and small employer plan tax credit	-4,021	-14,378
Extend the American opportunity tax credit	-33,806	-93,596
Exclude forgiven student loan debt from income	-	-
Tax capital gains and dividends of certain taxpayers at 20%	-45,235	-123,671
Tax Cuts for Businesses	-46,630	-116,381
Eliminate taxation of capital gains on investments in qualified small business stock	-	-5,417

---

[22] Under current law, the estate tax exemption will drop to $1 million in 2013, the top rate reverts to 60%, the state death deduction reverts to a credit, and the portability option for spouses expires.

Provision	2012-2016	2012-2021
Enhance and permanently extend the research and experimentation tax credit	-41,785	-106,278
Tax credit for investment in advanced energy property	-3,820	-3,661
Tax credit for energy efficient commercial building expenditures	-1,025	-1,025
Incentives to Promote Regional Growth	**-4,703**	**-5,253**
Extend and modify the New Markets Tax Credit (NMTC)	-858	-1,870
Reform and expand the Build American Bonds	-13	-28
Reform and expand the Low-Income Housing Tax Credit (LIHTC) program	-176	-872
Designate growth zones	-3,656	-2,483
Continue Certain Expiring Provisions Through Calendar Year 2012	**-21,682**	**-22,321**
Pay for Alternative Minimum Tax (AMT) Relief	**113,884**	**321,291**
Other Revenue Changes and Loophole Closers:	**166,153**	**356,481**
Reform treatment of financial institutions and products	11,304	33,216
Reinstate Superfund taxes	9,575	20,819
Increase the oil spill liability trust fund financing rate by one cent	219	451
Make the unemployment tax permanent	7,217	15,015
Repeal LIFO method of accounting for inventories	21,188	52,880
Repeal the gain limitation for dividends received in reorganization exchanges	377	849
Reform U.S. international tax system:		
- *Defer deduction of expenses related to deferred income*	25,017	37,665
- *Reform foreign tax credit*	22,243	51,444
- *Tax currently excess returns associated with transfers of intangibles offshore*	9,848	20,831
- *Limit shifting of income through intangible property transfers*	448	1,668
- *Disallow the deduction for excess non-taxed reinsurance premiums paid to affiliates*	1,103	2,614
- *Limit earnings stripping by expatriated entities*	1,780	4,222
Reform treatment of Insurance Companies and Products:		
- *Modify rules that apply to the sales of life insurance contracts*	344	1,243
- *Modify dividends-received deduction for life insurance company separate accounts*	2,368	5,146
- *Expand pro-rate interest expense disallowance for corporate-owned life insurance (COLI)*	979	7,691
Eliminate fossil-fuel tax preferences:		
- *Eliminate coal preferences*	1,108	2,579
- *Eliminate oil and gas preferences*	22,867	43,612
Tax carried (profits) interest as ordinary income	10,086	14,807

Provision	2012-2016	2012-2021
Deny deduction for punitive damages	127	312
Repeal lower-of-cost-or-market inventory accounting method	5,489	8,168
Simplify the tax code	148	407
Reduce the tax gap and make reforms:		
- *Expand information reporting*	*-3,255*	*-8,005*
- *Improve compliance by businesses*	*3,281*	*8,774*
- *Strengthen tax administration*	*104*	*263*
- *Expand penalties*	*138*	*327*
Estate tax	7,510	19,539
Total	115,094	280,254

Source: Office of Management and Budget , *Budget of the United States Government, Fiscal Year 2012: Summary Tables*, Washington, DC, February 14, 2011, pp. 183-187, at http://www.whitehouse.gov/sites/default/files/omb/budget/fy2012/assets/tables.pdf.

Author Contact Information

Mark P. Keightley, Coordinator
Analyst in Economics
mkeightley@crs.loc.gov, 7-1049

James M. Bickley
Specialist in Public Finance
jbickley@crs.loc.gov, 7-7794

Gary Guenther
Analyst in Public Finance
gguenther@crs.loc.gov, 7-7742

Thomas L. Hungerford
Specialist in Public Finance
thungerford@crs.loc.gov, 7-6422

Steven Maguire
Specialist in Public Finance
smaguire@crs.loc.gov, 7-7841

Donald J. Marples
Section Research Manager
dmarples@crs.loc.gov, 7-3739

Molly F. Sherlock
Specialist in Public Finance
msherlock@crs.loc.gov, 7-7797

Key Policy Staff

Area of Expertise	Name	Phone	E-mail
Budget, Debt Limits, Deficit Financing, Treasury Bonds	Andrew Austin	7-6552	aaustin@crs.loc.gov
Tax Gap and Tax Reform	James Bickley	7-7794	jbickley@crs.loc.gov
Small Business Tax, Research and Development Tax Policy	Gary Guenther	7-7742	gguenther@crs.loc.gov

Area of Expertise	Name	Phone	E-mail
Tax Expenditures, Capital Gains Tax, Trust Funds, Individual Retirement Accounts	Tom Hungerford	7-6422	thungerford@crs.loc.gov
Housing Tax, Education Tax, Business and Corporate Tax,	Mark Keightley	7-1049	mkeightley@crs.loc.gov
Budget, Debt Limits, Deficit Financing, Treasury Bonds	Mindy Levit	7-7792	mlevit@crs.loc.gov
State and Local Finance, AMT, Estate Tax, Private Activity Bonds	Steve Maguire	7-7841	smaguire@crs.loc.gov
Energy Tax, Tax Exempt Organizations, Corporate Tax	Molly Sherlock	7-7797	msherlock@crs.loc.gov

www.ingramcontent.com/pod-product-compliance
Lightning Source LLC
Chambersburg PA
CBHW082203290526
45794CB00008B/3404